MARGARET AND THE MOON
HOW MARGARET HAMILTON SAVED THE FIRST LUNAR LANDING

BY DEAN ROBBINS

ILLUSTRATED BY LUCY KNISLEY

ALFRED A. KNOPF ⚞ NEW YORK

To friend and mentor Marietta Zacker —D.R.
To Hazel, brilliant niece —L.K.

Acknowledgments
Thank you to Margaret Hamilton for generously sharing her life story
and patiently explaining the technical details of her work.
And thank you to Julia Maguire for her expert editorial guidance. —D.R.

THIS IS A BORZOI BOOK PUBLISHED BY ALFRED A. KNOPF

Text copyright © 2017 by Dean Robbins
Jacket art and interior illustrations copyright © 2017 by Lucy Knisley
Photographs courtesy of Margaret Hamilton and NASA
All rights reserved. Published in the United States by Alfred A. Knopf,
an imprint of Random House Children's Books, a division of Penguin Random House LLC, New York.
Knopf, Borzoi Books, and the colophon are registered trademarks of Penguin Random House LLC.

Visit us on the Web! randomhousekids.com
Educators and librarians, for a variety of teaching tools, visit us at RHTeachersLibrarians.com

Library of Congress Cataloging-in-Publication Data
Names: Robbins, Dean, author. | Knisley, Lucy, illustrator.
Title: Margaret and the Moon : how Margaret Hamilton saved the first lunar landing / Dean Robbins ; illustrated by Lucy Knisley.
Description: First edition. | New York : Alfred A. Knopf, 2017.
Identifiers: LCCN 2015039930 | ISBN 978-0-399-55185-7 (trade) | ISBN 978-0-399-55186-4 (lib. bdg.) | ISBN 978-0-399-55187-1 (ebook)
Subjects: LCSH: Hamilton, Margaret Heafield, 1936– —Juvenile literature. | Project Apollo (U.S.)—History—Juvenile literature.
| Computer software developers—United States—Biography—Juvenile literature. | Computer programmers—United States—Biography—Juvenile literature.
| Women scientists—United States—Biography—Juvenile literature. | Scientists—United States—Biography—Juvenile literature. | Moon—Juvenile literature.
Classification: LCC QA76.2.H36 R63 2017 | DDC 629.45/4092—dc23

The illustrations in this book were created using ink and paper and colored in Adobe Photoshop.
MANUFACTURED IN CHINA   May 2017   10 9 8 7 6 5 4 3 2 1   First Edition
Random House Children's Books supports the First Amendment and celebrates the right to read.

MARGARET HAMILTON LOVED TO SOLVE PROBLEMS.

SHE CAME UP WITH IDEAS
NO ONE HAD EVER THOUGHT OF BEFORE.

WHY WERE THERE ONLY **DADDY** LONGLEGS?
MARGARET HAD A SOLUTION.

SHE WOULD CALL SOME OF THEM
MOMMY LONGLEGS, TOO.

WHY DIDN'T GIRLS PLAY BASEBALL?

MARGARET HAD A SOLUTION.

SHE WOULD JOIN THE TEAM HERSELF.

READING...

MUSIC...

ART...

AND *ESPECIALLY* MATHEMATICS.

SHE LEARNED AS MUCH AS SHE COULD ABOUT ADDITION
AND SUBTRACTION, MULTIPLICATION AND DIVISION.

MARGARET'S FATHER WAS A POET AND PHILOSOPHER WHO TALKED TO HER ABOUT THE UNIVERSE.

SHE ASKED ABOUT HOW THE PLANETS MOVED.

WHEN THE GALAXIES FORMED.

WHY THE STARS SHONE.

SHE GAZED AT THE NIGHT SKY IN WONDER.

HOW MANY MILES TO THE MOON?

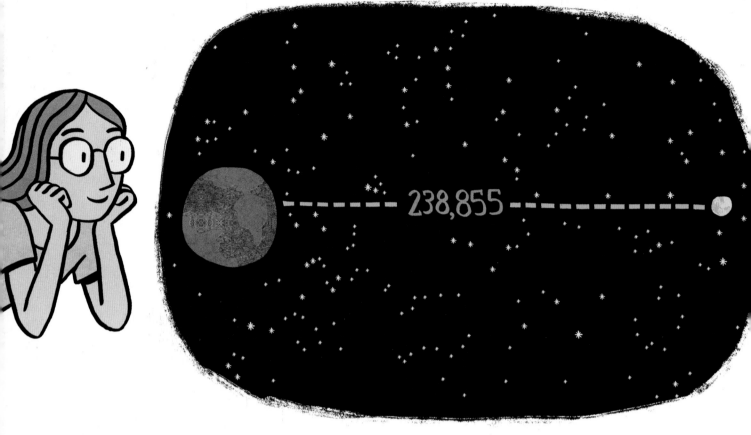

HOW MANY MILES DOES IT TRAVEL AROUND THE EARTH?

MARGARET BEGAN SOLVING HARDER AND HARDER MATH PROBLEMS.

IT WAS FUN WORKING HER WAY THROUGH THE STEPS.

SHE LIKED MOVING AROUND X'S AND Y'S IN ALGEBRA.

SHE LIKED MEASURING CIRCLES AND TRIANGLES IN GEOMETRY.

SHE LIKED STUDYING CURVES IN CALCULUS.

MARGARET COULD USE THIS NEW INVENTION
TO ANSWER SO MANY QUESTIONS ABOUT THE UNIVERSE!

SHE EXPERIMENTED WITH WRITING INSTRUCTIONS—OR CODE—
THAT TOLD THE MACHINE WHAT TO DO.

THE CODE WAS CALLED SOFTWARE,
AND MARGARET CALLED HERSELF A SOFTWARE ENGINEER.

SHE STARTED WITH SOMETHING SIMPLE:
ASKING THE COMPUTER TO ADD AND SUBTRACT, MULTIPLY AND DIVIDE.

MARGARET TAUGHT HERSELF TO WRITE CODE THAT PERFORMED
MORE AND MORE COMPLICATED TASKS.

SHE PROGRAMMED COMPUTERS
TO TRACK AIRPLANES THROUGH THE CLOUDS...

AND EVEN TO PREDICT THE WEATHER.

SHE MADE THEM DO THINGS
THEY HAD NEVER DONE BEFORE.

IN 1964, MARGARET GOT INTERESTED IN AN EXCITING PROJECT FOR NASA, THE NATIONAL AERONAUTICS AND SPACE ADMINISTRATION.

THEIR SCIENTISTS WERE WORKING
ON THE HARDEST PROBLEM HUMANS EVER TRIED TO SOLVE—
FLYING PEOPLE TO THE MOON!

COULD MARGARET USE COMPUTERS TO GET THE ASTRONAUTS...

...238,855 MILES THERE...

...AND 238,855 MILES BACK?

$$r_1 = \sqrt{D^2 + r_2^2 - 2Dr_2 \cos\lambda_1}$$

$$\sin\gamma_1 = \frac{}{r_1} \sin\lambda_1 -$$

$$Y_0 = v_1 - v_2 \quad \gamma_1 - \omega_M \Delta t$$

SHE CONVINCED NASA'S LEADERS TO LET HER TRY.

MARGARET THOUGHT OF EVERYTHING
THAT COULD HAPPEN ON A TRIP TO THE MOON.

WOULD THE
SPACECRAFT
GO OFF COURSE?

WOULD IT LOSE
POWER?

WOULD AN ASTRONAUT
MAKE A MISTAKE?

MARGARET WROTE CODE TO TELL THE COMPUTERS
HOW TO SOLVE THESE PROBLEMS.

SHE WORKED HER WAY
THROUGH THE STEPS
JUST AS SHE USED TO
DO IN MATH CLASS.

SOON MARGARET BECAME DIRECTOR OF SOFTWARE
PROGRAMMING FOR NASA'S PROJECT APOLLO,
LEADING DOZENS OF SCIENTISTS.

WITH APOLLO 11, NASA WOULD FINALLY
TRY TO PUT PEOPLE ON THE MOON.

HAD MARGARET THOUGHT OF
EVERYTHING THAT COULD GO WRONG
WITH A LUNAR LANDING?

SHE CHECKED HER CODE
AGAIN TO MAKE SURE.

MARGARET FOLLOWED ALONG FROM A CONTROL ROOM, AND THE WHOLE WORLD WATCHED ON TELEVISION.

FOR FOUR DAYS, THE SPACECRAFT DREW NEARER TO THE MOON.
THE LUNAR MODULE, NAMED THE EAGLE,
SPLIT OFF TO MAKE THE LANDING.

BUT WITH MINUTES LEFT TO GO, AN ASTRONAUT
ENTERED A COMMAND AND THE MASTER ALARM BUZZED.

THE EAGLE'S COMPUTER STARTED
PERFORMING TOO MANY TASKS.

OVERLOAD!
OVERLOAD!

YIKES!

THE CONTROL ROOM PANICKED.
THE MOON LANDING WAS IN DANGER!

EVERYONE LOOKED AT MARGARET.
HAD SHE PREPARED FOR THIS PROBLEM?

OF COURSE!

MARGARET'S CODE MADE THE COMPUTER IGNORE THE EXTRA TASKS AND FOCUS ON THE LANDING.

IT BROUGHT THE EAGLE CLOSER TO THE MOON'S SURFACE.

LATER THAT NIGHT, THE EAGLE'S HATCH OPENED.
MARGARET HELD HER BREATH.
ARMSTRONG TOOK THE FIRST STEP ON THE MOON.

THE WHOLE WORLD CELEBRATED IN FRONT OF THEIR TELEVISIONS.

MARGARET WALKED OUTSIDE, SMILING.

HER CODE HAD HELPED THE ASTRONAUTS GET TO THE MOON,
AND SHE KNEW IT WOULD HELP GET THEM HOME SAFELY.

AS ALWAYS, SHE GAZED AT THE NIGHT SKY IN WONDER.

AUTHOR'S NOTE

As a child in the 1930s and '40s, Margaret Hamilton (who was born Margaret Heafield) wondered why girls and boys weren't treated the same. She wondered about a lot of other things, too. Why is the universe there? What is the meaning of life? How could she do something important when she grew up? Her father always took her questions seriously, talking with her about religion, philosophy, and science. He made her believe she could be anything she wanted, which was uncommon at a time when girls had limited opportunities to pursue their dreams.

Margaret liked using her imagination to solve problems, and she often thought up unusual solutions that really worked. Her fearlessness led her to become a pioneer in programming computers after she graduated from college. At the time, the job had no name, so she made one up: software engineer. She was one of the only female computer scientists of the 1950s and '60s.

People didn't know much about computers then, so Margaret had to figure them out herself. She got experience by predicting weather for the Massachusetts Institute of Technology (MIT). After that, she became the director of software programming for an MIT laboratory working on Project Apollo for the National Aeronautics and Space Administration (NASA). She was excited about sending astronauts to the moon, and she knew she and her team could help.

In 1969, Margaret became a hero of the *Apollo 11* mission. Due to an error on the astronauts' checklist, a switch ended up in the wrong position and a computer overloaded. It looked like the lunar module might have to turn back—and it might even crash! But Margaret's brilliant programming allowed the computer to zero in on its most important task: landing the spacecraft safely on the moon.

After leaving NASA, Margaret started software companies and invented technology that made computers work even better. In 2003, she won NASA's Exceptional Space Act Award for her groundbreaking contributions to the United States space program. It came with a check for $37,200, the largest award to an individual in NASA's history. The Exceptional Space Act Award recognized Margaret's extraordinary scientific achievement, saying that "Apollo lives on today, continuing to impact the modern world in part through the many innovations created and championed by Ms. Hamilton."

BIBLIOGRAPHY

"Aiming High." *Earlhamite,* Summer 2004.

Campbell-Kelly, Martin, and William Aspray, Nathan Ensmenger, and Jeffrey R. Yost. *Computer: A History of the Information Machine.* Boulder, CO: Westview Press, 2013.

Chandler, David. "Recalling the 'Giant Leap.'" *MIT News,* July 17, 2009.

Johnson, Carolyn Y. "Scientist Reflects on Being at Vanguard of Software, Space Travel." *Boston Globe,* April 27, 2015.

McMillan, Robert. "Her Code Got Humans to the Moon—And Invented Software Itself." *Wired,* October 13, 2015.

Murray, Charles, and Catherine Bly Cox. *Apollo: The Race to the Moon.* New York: Simon & Schuster, 1989.

Sagan, Carl. *Cosmos.* New York: Random House, 1980.

Schneider, Caitlin. "Meet the Woman Behind the Apollo Project." *Mental Floss,* June 10, 2015.

ADDITIONAL READING

Aguilar, David A. *Space Encyclopedia: A Tour of Our Solar System and Beyond.* New York: National Geographic Children's Books, 2013.

Gibson, Karen Bush. *Women in Space: 23 Stories of First Flights, Scientific Missions, and Gravity-Breaking Adventures.* Chicago: Chicago Review Press, 2014.

Simon, Seymour. *The Moon.* New York: Simon & Schuster Books for Young Readers, 2003.

Thimmesh, Catherine. *Team Moon: How 400,000 People Landed Apollo 11 on the Moon.* Boston: HMH Books for Young Readers, 2015.

MARGARET WITH HER CODE

Photo courtesy of NASA

MARGARET IN COSTUME

Photo courtesy of Margaret Hamilton © Eliezer Partington

MARGARET AT MIT

Photo courtesy of Margaret Hamilton